The Essential Handbook for Effective Human Service Professionals

Written By:

Tim Nolan, M.S., M.S.

First published by Dog Ear Publishing
4010 W. 86th Street, Ste H
Indianapolis, IN 46268
www.dogearpublishing.net

ISBN: 978-1-4575-1987-1

This book is printed on acid-free paper.

Printed in the United States of America

To those that continually aspire to make a difference
in the lives of others.

Table of Contents

Preface

The human services field is at a critical juncture. Organizations are struggling to not only meet client needs but also meet and exceed outcome measures in order to sustain their funding. This has also placed a considerable burden on the workforce-workers have to balance client care along with meeting necessary outcome measures, which do not seem to coincide with the primary purpose of helping their clients.

Human service organizations continue to struggle to effectively hire and retain staff due to increased work demands, budget cuts, staff shortages, and lack of staff development opportunities. Still, many continue to enter the human services due to the rewarding feeling of helping others to succeed. The fact remains that many professionals entering the field are not equipped with the practical support and tools needed.

The Essential Handbook for Effective Human Service Professionals was written to help provide new and experienced workers with the skills and perspective necessary to maximize client care and professional performance. This book would not be possible without the assistance of hundreds of supervisors, managers, and directors that provided their feedback during the various trainings that I conducted during the past year; to you I extend a sincere thank you.

After touring the country and working with over one thousand human service managers, it became apparent that a handbook would be needed for workers in the same way that *The Essential Handbook for Human Service Leaders* was written. As such,

I went about assessing vital competencies for effective staff performance and came up with 21 that would provide information and guidance on how to excel and navigate in this ambiguous, stressful, yet highly rewarding field.

It is my hope that you find the information helpful and easy to refer to.

Regards,

Tim Nolan

Introduction

The Essential Handbook for Effective Human Service Professionals has a clear and concise focus: to provide workers in the human services (i.e. child welfare case managers, juvenile probation officers, family service specialists, child protective investigators, and various others non-management personnel) with the skills, strategies, and perspective needed to maximize client care, optimize professional development and enhance worker commitment to the agency. Moreover, this book helps to empower workers to maximize their leadership within the organization and community. In all, this book reviews 21 vital competencies needed to be an effective professional in the human services.

Human service organizations often struggle to adequately define vital competencies needed for workers to be successful due to limited budgets, staff shortages, and high workloads.

Still, it is up to the worker to utilize the information provided and work through any and all barriers to help clients. Employee turnover is high in some segments of the human services. Common complaints include but are not limited to: low pay, high workloads, personal impact of the work, not agreeing with their manager, etc.

Still, there are over one million human service professionals in the United States and this number is expected to rapidly grow over the next 10 years due to the evolving needs of our population. *The Essential Handbook for Effective Human Service Professionals* fills a critical void in the field in that it provides clear examples and strategies to enhance client care and worker growth and credibility. Regardless of the reader's experience level there are useful tools available that will take your performance to the next level. Above all, choose to be the professional that finds a way to make it happen for clients.

CHAPTER ONE

Client Engagement and Advocacy

Positive client engagement and advocacy is at the heart of being an effective human service professional. Clients come in contact with human service organizations due to needing assistance and expect to interact with a professional that will actively work to resolve their issue(s). Even though there may be barriers to engaging clients, effective human service professionals see opportunities in even the most challenging of situations. The better the relationship is with your client(s), the better the treatment outcome.

Effective Client Engagement Includes

- Building rapport. This starts with the initial contact with a client/family. Effective human service professionals are experts at forming, building, and maintaining quality relationships with clients. This is a core skill and one that professionals need to ensure that it is a clear strength for them.
  - For example, a family services specialist with Head Start meets with a family and warmly greets them as they refer to them by their proper name (Mr. and Mrs. Smith). The professional appears happy to meet with them and takes the time necessary to answer their questions. It is important to not rush the clients and be mindful that their initial impression of the entire program is mostly going to come from their interaction with you. This is why it is

important to always be mindful of the impact that we have on our clients and the opinion they will form of the agency.

- Showing interest. Even though your schedule will be constantly full, there is always time to show interest in clients. It is important that we ask follow up questions and actively participate in all interactions with clients. Working in the human services is about relationships.
  - A foster care case manager meets with her foster parents monthly and while this is routine their approach is not. They spend the time needed to make small talk with their families and are knowledgeable about events going on in their lives through follow up questions that they ask. In turn, the foster parents are much more likely to willingly offer up information due to the positive relationship that they have. Moreover, the foster parents feel like their worker looks out for them and cares about them as people, not just objects and bed space for children.
- Ask questions. This is a skill that is vital for all human service professionals. Asking questions help to maximize relationships with clients by obtaining information as well as helping the client feel that they are unique and cared for. By making this a clear strength you will stand out as a professional.
  - Reasons to ask questions
    - Create clarity
    - Improve relationships
    - Inspire others to reflect on their behaviors and choices
    - Challenge assumptions
    - Encourage clients to take ownership of behaviors
  - Examples of questions to ask
    - Who watches your child when you are at work?
    - What do you think you can do differently?

- When was the last time your child when to the doctor?
- Where are the cleaning supplies kept in your home?
- Why do you think that happened?
- How is your relationship with your supervisor?
- Empathy. Every client has a unique story and experience that led them to receiving services. It is not up to the worker to judge the client but to understand their story so that they can provide the best service possible. Effective human service professionals place themselves in their client's situation to genuinely see their point of view.
- For example, you may be assigned a family after losing custody of their child due to physical abuse. Your initial reaction may be to judge the parents for hurting their child but after taking the time to learn about the parents you realize that both of them grew up in abusive households and they were only using the methods that they thought to be appropriate and normal. While it does not excuse their behavior, it does provide context as to why they behaved the way they did and allows you to work with them to learn new skills.
- Support. Support is a term that has many meanings for the client as well as for the professional. Be sure to work with the client to define what support means for them as well as balancing what support you think the client needs versus what their actual needs are in the situation.
  - How to define support
    - "What does support look like for you?"
    - "How can I support you during this difficult time?"
- Acknowledge the difficulty of the situation. Clients will become involved with your agency for a variety of reasons- voluntary or involuntary (i.e. court mandated). It is recommended to acknowledge the difficulty of participating in

services-this can go a long way to the client feeling that you are seeing them as a human being and not just a number.

- Spend sufficient time with clients. There are more clients seeking services compared to decades past and this has placed a heavy burden on organizations. However, this is not a concern for clients. Just like you would want the full attention of your physician when you go to see them for medical care, clients deserve your full attention and extra time, if needed.
  - For example, Janice had a staff meeting scheduled for 2:00 p.m. but a client interview was running late. Janice spent the extra time with her client rather than rushing the interview. Even though her supervisor was initially upset that she was late to the meeting Janice's supervisor was fine with her being late after she explained why.
- Strengths based. All clients have strengths. While there will be some that are highly challenging to engage it is far easier to build rapport when workers focus on the strengths of the clients. By strengths, the worker should focus on what the client is doing well or what they are good at. Many clients needing assistance may not demonstrate many strengths on the surface, but effective professionals help their clients uncover them.
- Active listening. Steven Covey put it best when he stated "Seek first to understand, then to be understood." This also applies to client engagement. It is vital that clients know you are listening to them and fully hear what they are telling you. Regardless of how busy you may be, clients deserve your full attention.
  - Barriers to effective listening include:
    - Being preoccupied with our own thoughts
    - Jumping to conclusions before the client is finished speaking
    - Selectively listening to what the client is speaking about
    - Allowing our own emotions to get in the way-anxious, tired, etc.
    - Being in a hurry

- Effective listening skills include:
  - Being present
  - Restating what the client says
  - Affirm the client's experiences-acknowledge their struggles and the strengths that they possess
  - Be genuine
- Clear expectations: professionals know how the system works and how to access services but clients often struggle with this. Effective human service professionals do not assume the client knows how the process works; they take the time to ensure that every client fully understands what is expected of them and how to ask for help.
- Creating a partnership: clients need to see the professional as someone that cares about their wellbeing and is invested in their treatment. Creating a partnership involves:
  - Obtaining client commitment to be an active participant
  - The client and the professional mutually work on and agree to goals for the client
  - Clients see the human services professional that has skills and expertise to offer them-the professional will help them to develop concrete skills that they can use

Engaging Difficult and/or Resistant Clients

- Clients may present as resistant and difficult for a variety of reasons including:
  - Involuntarily having to participate in services
  - Not seeing the benefit of participating in services
  - Not wanting to change
  - Not willing to do the work necessary to change their behavior
  - Mental health issues
- Keys to effectively engaging difficult and/or resistant clients:
  - Clear expectations

- Be respectful and professional at all times (i.e. do not raise your voice, remain calm, and focus on the issues rather than their behavior).
- Be consistent-do not avoid them because of their issues
- Focus on behaviors and outcomes ("How do you think that will help you to obtain employment?"
- Look for small victories (i.e. small compromises like time to complete the home visit)
- Always be mindful of the potential for physical aggression on the part of the client and protect yourself as necessary.

Other Important Aspects Related to Effectively Engaging Clients

- Do not judge clients: human service professionals will, over the course of their career, encounter a wide variety of clients and client behaviors. It is important to approach each situation from the standpoint of understanding the circumstances surrounding needing assistance and how you can help. It is not up to the worker to judge the client.
- Be mindful of your values and beliefs and do not allow them to interfere with providing high quality client care:
    - For example, a child protection services worker may go to a client's home and see that it is dirty with evidence of a few roaches on the ground. While most would agree that this is not an ideal living environment it may not lead to a child being removed due to environmental hazards. However, if the worker was raised in a much different environment they may equate poor with being a poor parent, which is not the case.
- Be aware of your emotional state when working with clients. Working in the human services can be difficult at times but clients should never know if you are experiencing personal issues. Maintain professionalism at all times, especially if the client is being disrespectful.
- Agree to disagree. If you do not agree with a client consider using comments like "That is one way to look at it". You do

not need to respond to every comment that a client makes and sometimes clients make comments to see what your reaction will be. Effective human service professionals remain in the middle as much as possible and focus on the important issues impacting the clients.

Client Advocacy Involves

- Always acting in the client's best interest
    - Use phrases like, "This is in the client's best interest because…" to effectively help you make your case to management when needed. It is important to do what is best for the client, not what is best for the professionals.
    - Keep the client informed of progress, challenges and/or barriers that you are experiencing.
    - Provide the client with all available choices, fully explain them, and help educate them on the best options for them based on their circumstances as well as initiating a pro and con discussion.

Going Above and Beyond

Michelle is an adoptions worker for a county organization. She prides herself on having an excellent relationship with her clients and it shows. Her supervisor and agency conduct frequent quality calls to clients and they consistently report how much they enjoy working with Michelle. Further, the clients report that Michelle always takes the time to answer their questions, walk them through the adoption process in a clear and concise manner, and is always available to answer the questions. One family noted that even though they were not selected for the child that they had applied for Michelle was there afterwards to provide support to them and help them through the process.

**Strong client relationships
are the foundation for
excellent service delivery.**

CHAPTER TWO

Organization and Time Management

If you ask supervisors a key skill that workers need to possess in order to be effective and most of them will tell you time management and organization skills. There are many demands placed on human service professionals and this is why effective time management and organization are vital to your success. Those that are highly successful are the ones that can effectively balance multiple projects at once and do so with a high degree of skill.

Tips to Maximize Organizational and Time Management Skills

- Prioritize: not every task is a priority. For example, completing a court report that is due today is more important than completing a clothing voucher for a client that can be done by the end of the week. It is important to schedule your activity around the most critical work first. Time spent on noncritical tasks will take you away from what is vital and put you behind.
- Time management tools: whether you use a calendar, Microsoft Outlook, or your smart phone to stay on top of your assignments and tasks select a mode that works best for you. Either way, it is important to have a method for writing down when important reports and home visits are due.
  - Leslie uses her Blackberry to look at her availability and to synch her schedule and appointments with

her work computer. Whenever something comes up she reviews her availability to ensure that she has time or can offer alternatives to her clients. This also works well for her supervisor since she can readily see Leslie's schedule and can plan meetings around her availability.

- Do not procrastinate: waiting until the last minute never works out well-for you, the agency, or the client. As such, be as proactive as possible.

  - For example, Mindy made it a point to have all of her home visits completed by the third week of the month. She would schedule all of them the first three weeks of the month which allowed her an extra week in case the visit did not occur. This also allowed her to schedule extra visits if needed and to complete all of her monthly paperwork the last week.

- Know when you are most productive: we all have time in the day when we are at our best. For some it can be in the beginning of the morning or right before lunch. While for others it may be in the afternoon. Either way, know when you are at your best and when you will be most focused to complete paperwork, make phone calls, etc.

- Be mindful of activities that decrease your productivity: various research studies have estimated that companies lose billions of dollars every year to internet surfing. With the internet only a click away (on your phone or computer) it is important to know there is a place and a time for this activity. Having a designated time to surf the internet and make personal phone calls will increase your productivity.

- Set time limits for each activity: knowing how much time you are spending on each task is very important, especially if you find yourself spending too much time devoted to certain tasks. Writing a court report may take an hour while calling your clients may take 30 minutes. Either way, it is best to know how long each activity takes and to schedule this time (but build in time for interruptions).

- Map out tasks for the week and for the day: before you start your week it is a good practice to review what is due for the week before you go to work on Monday. This allows you to be mentally prepared and to complete any outstanding work beforehand.
- Ask for help/delegate: a common issue with many human service professionals is reluctance to ask for help, especially when there is a high volume of work to be completed. With burnout and high workloads a constant issue in the field, it is vital to be able to ask a peer or your supervisor for assistance when needed. Asking for help is a sign of strength, not weakness.
  - For example, John was going on vacation for a week and needed assistance completing a couple of home visits by the end of the week. He had already scheduled to work late three nights that week but instead of adding another night he asked two peers if they could complete one home visit each, which they agreed to do. This saved John precious time so that he could complete other work before going out.
- Multitasking: there are always opportunities throughout the day to complete little tasks while you are waiting.
  - For example, Dawn responded to several emails while waiting for her court case to be heard.
- Long hours do not mean high productivity: be mindful of the hours that you are spending on the job. While working 40 hours a week is ideal, it is not the norm in the human services. However, if one is routinely working 60 hours a week they need to evaluate their work practices and scheduling.

Going Above and Beyond

Juan always completes his work on time if not early. He uses his smart phone to keep track of his appointments and schedules a day and time each week to complete his notes. He knows when reports are due and sets reminders of when important tasks need to be completed. Further, his schedule is on his work calendar, which makes it easy for his supervisor to see what he has planned and to schedule meetings around his availability.

Remain organized to reduce stress and maximize professional credibility.

CHAPTER THREE

Work with a High Sense of Urgency/Take Initiative

Effective human service professionals work with a high sense of urgency and take initiative to complete tasks with minimal direction from management. Working with a high sense of urgency and taking initiative increase your credibility as a human service professional with clients and within your organization.

By definition, working with a high sense of urgency means not waiting until later in the week to complete a task for a client when it can be completed that day. It means completing the referral as soon as the need arises rather than waiting on being told or reminded to complete it. Effective human service professionals work with a high sense of urgency to break through barriers to successfully meet client needs because they are depending on you to advocate for them.

Taking initiative refers to working independently to complete tasks. Collaborating with your peers and supervisor are very important, but not always necessary. It is essential for professionals to proactively address issues without prompts from their supervisor. Additionally, taking initiative means using your judgment to proactively address client issues.

Working with a High Sense of Urgency

- Set priorities. As mentioned previously, organized professionals set priorities and realize what needs to be completed immediately versus what can wait for a day or two. While

not every issue is a high priority, highly effective professionals quickly address issues that need to be completed,
regardless of priority level. A few examples include:

- Brian's court report was not due until Friday but he
  wanted to complete it as soon as possible so that his
  supervisor could review it and give the department
  attorney adequate time before court to make recommendations. Brian liked to complete his work
  early so that he could focus on more pressing client
  needs.
- As soon as the treatment team meeting concluded
  Leslie went straight to her office to complete the
  family therapy referral. She knew that if she waited
  until later in the day other issues would arise and she
  wanted to have services begin as soon as possible for
  the family.
- After completing supervision with her manager
  Kelly went straight to her office to begin working
  on the follow ups that her supervisor had given her
  during their meeting.
- Responding to clients and internal team mem-
  bers/management: Highly effective human service professionals quickly respond in a timely manner. For example:
  - Returning client phone calls within one business
    day, sooner if possible.
  - Responding to inquiries from management within
    the same hour, if possible. Due to the high level of
    email communication which frequently occurs in
    organizations, it is important to be very responsive
    to your manager as well as from other individuals in
    management. Waiting several hours to respond to
    an email can cause the worker to lose credibility and
    not provide adequate information to solve the
    problem.
- It is important to take into account that individuals are rely-
  ing on you to follow through for them. When one waits
  until the last minute to complete a task it does not allow for
  services to begin in a timely manner and can potentially

delay a larger outcome from occurring (i.e. family reunification, speech therapy to begin for a child, etc.).

- The benefits to working with a high degree of urgency are many and include, but not limited to:
  - Timely resolution of client issues
  - Greater time to focus on more pressing client concerns
  - Enhanced credibility within the agency and community as a "make it happen" professional
  - Consideration for promotional opportunities

Taking Initiative

- Proactively anticipate potential client issues and be one step ahead. For example:
  - Sally had worked with Johan for several months and knew that when he was released from his inpatient program he would need various community supports to help him successfully transition back to being home. She initiated several referrals before his discharge including: a mentor, individual therapy, and finding out what activities he can participate in at school. Sally was especially proud that she addressed these concerns before her supervisor asked her what the long-term plan was for Johan.
  - Sandra had been in the classroom a few times to observe Marie and quickly realized that her classroom behavior may be impacted by a variety of issues. She quickly mobilized a meeting with the teaching staff and parents to see what could be done to proactively address her needs before her behavior severely impacted her academic performance.
  - Elaine had worked in the group home for a few months and realized that the residents would become restless in the afternoon after they came home from school. This led to an increase in restrictions so she took it upon herself to suggest a variety of activities to her supervisor that the home could do in the afternoon to reduce this issue.

Going Above and Beyond

Melissa likes to complete work as soon as it arises because she never knows what her day is going to be like. She had several reports due to her supervisor by the end of the week that she completed several days earlier. This allowed her supervisor to pinpoint an issue and have enough time to help Melissa address it before the court hearing. Melissa also takes pride in quickly addressing issues and being one step ahead in terms of proactively identifying issues and client needs.

**Effective professionals consistently
take initiative to address issues.**

CHAPTER FOUR

Communication Skills

The ability to effectively communicate is a vital component to being an effective human service professional. Possessing superior writing, speaking, and nonverbal communication skills not only allows for excellent client advocacy and care, but many advantages for career advancement. Many individuals struggle to communicate at a high level; this is why it is easy to distinguish oneself if this is an area of strength.

Developing Strong Communication Skills
- Writing: effective writing skills are not easily developed naturally but they can be with practice and commitment to improvement.
    - Reports: Be sure to write in a manner that is clear, concise, and factual. Also, be mindful of who your audience is when writing. For example, your writing will be different when sending an email to a coworker than when writing a court report that is read by a judge. Do not be too wordy with your writing and focus on providing the facts with the right amount of background information. Well written reports answer any potential questions the reader may have.
    - Documentation: As the saying goes, "If it is not documented it did not occur." It is very important to understand the seriousness of proper documentation. Consistent and concise documentation helps

to support the services being provided to a client and also support the worker in case an allegation of unethical behavior is made by the client or someone else. A few examples:

- Samantha did not always document all of her phone calls when parents called. She was always focused on addressing issues as they came up. However, when a parent reported that they spoke to Samantha several times about an incident occurring in the program, Samantha opened the child's file only to see a note made approximately two months ago-she failed to document several events that took place during the period in question. As such, the agency lost credibility with the parent and Samantha was eventually written up for not keeping her files up to date.

- Lisa was always very busy with her caseload but recognized the importance of keeping detailed notes to document client progress. As a child welfare case manager she was responsible for entering all documentation in the state database within 48 hours of an event. There was an occasion in which a client stated in court that Lisa did not complete a parenting referral for the client and she was able to demonstrate to the court the date that the referral was completed and who she spoke to at the agency. Her credibility within the agency and community were unquestioned due to her consistent ability to enter detailed notes in a timely manner.

- Emails: Emails are a large part of the communication process, especially within the organization and with other professionals. A few keys for effective email communication:
  - Be professional at all times. It is not uncommon for emails to start off as individual communication but others can quickly be added as they are copied on further responses and/or the email gets forwarded to others.

Be mindful of what the content of your message is and the tone in which your email may come across. Always write with the intention that your email could be read by others.

- Some professionals will minimize email usage and advise others to call them, especially in high profile situations-keep this in consideration.

- Avoid writing out of emotion. There will be times when situations occur which are frustrating but effective professionals are mindful of their emotional state. If you find yourself upset with someone assess if the email can be sent later in the day when you have had time to cool down and consider the best approach to the situation.

  - Sometimes consider having a coworker read over your email before sending it to gain another person's perspective.

- Find coworkers who write well and obtain copies of their work to use as guides. Also, take time to review journal articles and reports that you come across to use as guides to enhance your writing ability.

- Verbal communication:

  - Speak in a manner that clients can easily understand. Be sure to thoroughly review information in a way that makes it easy for them to comprehend. It is important to note that while the professional may review information on a regular basis (i.e. consents) it may be new to the client.

  - Ask questions. Stephen Covey in his book, *The Seven Habits of Highly Effective People*, wrote "Seek first to understand, then to be understood" this is a powerful statement that illustrates the importance of asking questions. The more questions you ask the more information you gain from the client and this will minimize assumptions. Additionally, asking questions allows you to maximize rapport with your clients.

- Avoid use of slang when speaking with your supervisor and coworkers. Speak in a measured and calm tone when possible. Remember that you are modeling positive behavior for your clients.
- Nonverbal communication:
  - Remain mindful of what your nonverbal behavior is communicating to your clients and coworkers. For example, facial expressions, crossed arms, etc. can all be potential signs that push others away.

Going Above and Beyond

Kenyatta was recently commended by her supervisor for her excellent writing skills on a court report. Kenyatta wrote a status update on one of her families and illustrated why it was being recommended for the family to have overnight visits with their children. The judge was impressed with the volume of supporting information provided and how the report was submitted several days before the court hearing to allow for the judge and attorney adequate time to review the information.

Use high quality communication skills to stand out and effectively advocate for client needs.

CHAPTER FIVE

Effectively Handling Conflict and Providing Feedback

Conflict is natural and healthy. Individuals have their own approach for handling conflict and it is important to recognize what your dominant approach is and how that impacts your ability to effectively work with clients and other professionals. Not addressing situations of conflict appropriately will reduce your professional credibility and lead to less than ideal client outcomes. See below to see what your dominant approach to handling conflict is-note that each approach is good to use in the right situation.

The Conflict Resolution Continuum

- Thomas-Kilmann identified five main styles to approaching and resolving conflict. Each approach is beneficial to use in the right situation.
  - Avoiders: this involves individuals who may deny that an issue exists. There may be times that they are aware of a situation but attempt to avert or ignore the conflict. Avoiders may find conflict anxiety provoking and seek to avoid it all costs. They also tend to be passive in nature. Avoidance is a good approach to use if the issue is not important and can be ignored (i.e. a client being a few minutes late for an appointment).

- Kirk struggled in working with one of his clients that he viewed as difficult and argumentative. He would set an appointment each month for this individual but would find other priorities to attend to whenever they arrived, leaving others to have to work with them. He did not look forward to seeing the client and avoided seeing them or answering their phone calls.
- Accommodators: are typically more concerned with the needs of others than themselves. Professionals who are accommodators may go out of their way to volunteer in completing tasks for clients versus helping them to become independent. They can be taken advantage of by savvy clients or coworkers. Accommodation is a good approach to use when keeping harmony is important (i.e. taking on extra tasks to help a mother who is close to be reunified with her child).
  - Kathy would frequently find herself in a situation of doing extra work for her clients. While she enjoyed her job she started becoming overwhelmed with the additional tasks she was taking on. Clients would frequently ask her to do extra things and rather than say no she would agree because she did not want to upset or disappoint clients.
- Competitors: individuals who present as competitors may be considered aggressive by peers or clients and often seek out win/lose arrangements. Relationships take on a low priority and the individual may have difficulty accepting feedback from others. They also may put forth great effort to be right. Competitors can be assertive given the right circumstance and this can be a good approach to use when a difficult decision needs to be made (violating a client who is not following the conditions of their probation).

- Compromisers: this type of approach is toward the middle of the continuum. The process of obtaining a compromise means that in some instances a win-win solution is not obtained. It is a good approach to use when attempting to resolve complex situations (i.e. a treatment team meeting involving multiple professionals and needing to reach a compromise to meet client needs).
- Collaborators: individuals who present with this approach actively encourages all parties to be involved in solving the problem. They see conflict as an opportunity. Collaboration allows both sides to get what they want and have negative feelings eliminated. All human service professionals should be adept at utilizing a collaboration approach to effectively resolving issues. Collaboration can be a time consuming process.

Providing Feedback

- The ability to consistently provide feedback to clients and coworkers is directly related to one's approach to handling conflict.
- Working with clients can frequently place you in situations of conflict, however one of the roles of a human service professional is to provide feedback to clients to help them gain insight of their behavior. If one tends to avoid conflict, for example, they are missing out on opportunities to provide vital feedback to clients and help them to make long-term gains.
- Examples of providing client feedback include:
  - Maria was consistently late for her weekly visit with her child. Her worker, Leigh, discussed this pattern of behavior with Maria and advised her that she would have to report it to the court. Maria began to be more punctual with future visits.
  - Damien was working with a youth to help him locate employment. He would review the youth's

applications before they were submitted and provided regular feedback to help improve his chances
of being selected for an interview.

- Sonia had a client who demonstrated a pattern of
testing positive for illegal substances during routine
drug screenings. Sonia took the opportunity to discuss the impact that failing a drug screen would have
on being reunified with their child as well as other
areas it may negatively impact them.

Going Above and Beyond

Vania works for a juvenile justice agency and has a caseload of
youth that she works with. She understands that each youth has
unique needs and approaches them a little differently. For some
youth she may be more accommodating while others she may be
stern and provide them with "straight talk". Still, she understands
that conflict is a natural part of the job, especially when a youth is
not adhering to the terms of their probation and may face further
consequences. She has found it best to proactively address conflict when it occurs because avoiding it will only make the problem worse.

**Strong and decisive professionals
proactively address conflict.**

CHAPTER SIX

Collaboration and Relationship Building

Building relationships with internal and external professionals is an integral part of maximizing your professional performance and meeting the needs of your clients. While all of the competencies in this book are important, the ability to build, maintain, and strengthen relationships is a critical skill. Those that can master this essential skill will have more resources available to meet client needs.

Building Strong Relationships with Internal Team Members

- Regardless if your organization is comprised of 10 or 500 employees, it is important to know the key personnel in each department. Working in the human services is rarely involves one individual, it is a team approach. As such, it is imperative to know which individuals can help you when needed. For example:
  - A foster parent reported that her board payment was inaccurate for several months in a row causing increased stress for her family that was struggling to care for a child with behavioral issues. Nivea has a good relationship with the fiscal department and was able to resolve the issue after speaking with Donna, who was not aware of the discrepancy in payment.

THE ESSENTIAL HANDBOOK FOR EFFECTIVE HUMAN SERVICE PROFESSIONALS   27

- Take initiative to learn about the different departments within your organization and how they help the agency in different ways. Depending on the size of your agency and services provided you may need the help of another department to resolve a client issue. Effective human service professionals are adept at navigating the organization and collaborating with key personnel to advocate for clients.
  - Luis was a new case manager with the agency and was eager to learn about his job but also about his coworkers. He made it a point to squeeze in a few moments within his orientation period to meet with and learn about the functions of each department. Even after the initial orientation he would make it a point to stop by periodically and say hello. His causal conversations helped him to learn about his coworkers and their duties, which made it easy for him to know where to go to when he encountered barriers.
- When issues arise, do not hesitate to seek input from team members in different departments (as long as their expertise is within the realm of the issue being addressed). There may be times when a treatment team meeting is scheduled and their presence can help provide vital information.

Building Strong Relationships with External Professionals

- With the human services being driven by strong team performance, working with external professionals and community providers is another important foundation to being a highly effective professional. It is not uncommon for a client to have simultaneous contact with multiple human service organizations. As such, having positive relationships with multiple providers and professionals is critical.
- Conduct research to find out what agencies are operating in your community. The first step is to be aware of what organizations exist and what services they provide.
- Find out the key personnel of those organizations (i.e. director, coordinator, intake supervisor, etc.).

- Make it a point to personally meet with the key individual(s) that may have a direct role in meeting the needs of your clients.
  - Juanita was in the area and made it a point to stop by a community services agency to see if Steve, intake supervisor, was available. Juanita introduced herself to Steve and mentioned her struggles to initiate services for her clients after a referral was made. Steve was surprised to hear about the issues and stated he would look into them. Juanita thanked him for his time and took down his contact information (cell phone number, email address, direct office number, etc.). Whenever Juanita encountered delays in initiating services for her clients she would call Steve to help problem solve the issue. This allowed her clients to receive services sooner than in the past.
- Once you identify and establish a relationship with a key contact at an agency do not overuse this relationship. If you call or email them too often it will reduce the effectiveness of the relationship. Be sure to only ask for assistance when the process is not working or if special attention is needed on a specific case.
- Pass on success stories (i.e. feedback of staff doing a good job) from time to time to your contacts. This helps to strengthen relationships and offers the other agency feedback. Moreover, it is a good opportunity to stay in contact.
- Ask clients if they are participating in other services so that, once consent is obtained you can gain information from that provider, if it is pertinent to the client's engagement with your agency. Often a client may only provide part of a story to a professional, which is why collaboration among external providers is vital.
- Once you are aware of other providers being involved with a client, be sure to communicate with them regularly. Try to initiate conference calls or in person meetings as needed. Whenever treatment meetings occur, be sure to invite all involved professionals so that the entire team is on the same page.

Going Above and Beyond

Jennifer learned quickly that building effective relationships would greatly enhance her ability to advocate for her clients. She made it a point to learn about the different departments within the agency and would frequently visit them so that they knew who she was. Her relationships with her coworkers have helped in numerous occasions when she experience challenges in resolving issues. Because of her knowledge of different departments, Jennifer is able to effectively advocate for her clients and is even a resource to her coworkers who ask for her advice.

Collaboration leads to excellent client care and professional relationships.

CHAPTER SEVEN

Critical Thinking and Problem Solving Skills

Professionals in the human services are constantly faced with situations where they must use problem solving and critical thinking skills. This typically entails having to think on your feet when situations do not work as planned, which can occur frequently. Highly effective professionals are adept at working through barriers and challenges to provide high quality services for their clients.

Maximizing Critical Thinking Skills
- There are many definitions of critical thinking but the main points involve:
  - Skillful conceptualization
  - Analyzing information
  - Applying information learned
  - Observation
  - Understanding of the how and why of a process
  - Reflection
  - Use of logic and reasoning
  - Use of reasoning to come to a thoughtful conclusion
  - Clarifies
  - Examines assumptions
  - Seeks evidence and facts to support conclusions
  - Being open minded

- Raises important questions
- Critical thinking also involves asking tough questions to obtain as much information as possible but doing so in a professional and tactful manner. Use questions to help obtain the answers that you are looking for without having to make assumptions.
  - Jeanne is usually the person who will ask a lot of questions during staff meetings. She likes to understand why decisions are being made and how certain decisions will impact her and her clients. She is not afraid to ask difficult questions and her peers frequently come to her after meetings and thank her for asking the questions that were on their minds.
  - Elaine is a detailed oriented case worker and wants to be sure that she has as much information as necessary in order to do her job. She will research various agency policies and procedures to ensure that she is following agency protocol to meet client needs. She even helped to change an agency policy when she noticed that there was a more efficient way to complete home visits and assisted in amending the policy.
  - Amanda was working with a client who had a history of domestic violence. Instead of assuming why the client engaged in specific behavior she would frequently ask him, "Why do you think you made that choice?"
- Effective critical thinking challenges the professional to fully understand the various processes that they engage in and to not always take the word of others. Trust information received but be sure to verify the accuracy to ensure your credibility is not negatively impacted.
  - Ryan was not sure of how to complete a specific referral for a client and asked a coworker for assistance. After receiving the needed information he also verified the accuracy of the material by double checking with his supervisor.

- Critical thinking requires the use of self-reflection. It is important to assess your thought process and challenge yourself to come up with the best solution to the problem, but from a rational viewpoint that is based on facts and minimizes emotion.
  - Dawn was in attendance at a treatment team meeting with several other professionals discussing what type of environment a child should be placed in. The foster parents were very attached to the child and did not want to see him leave their home even though he was presenting with increasingly unsafe behaviors. Other professionals provided information but from an emotional standpoint due to their relationship with the child. Dawn was able to redirect the group with her thoughtful points about why another placement would be in the child's best interest based on his behavior, risk to other children, academic needs, and therapeutic needs.
- Thinking versus knowing. Effective professionals minimize the use of assumptions and second hand information. This involves conducting your own research and due diligence to verify the accuracy of information so that you are certain what needs to be done versus thinking. This also helps if you encounter a situation and need to speak to your supervisor-demonstrating your knowledge of information and/or policies and procedures helps to build credibility as a professional.
  - A child protection worker met with a parent who was under investigation for allegations of child abuse due to domestic violence occurring in front of their child. The mother reported that she was no longer with the father. The worker wanted to double check before closing the case and decided to conduct an unannounced visit a few days later and found the father and his belongings at the house.
- Use critical thinking to see beyond the initial issue but several steps past the initial point. The easiest and most obvious solution is not always the best one.

- For example, if a child is removed from a school setting the easy answer may be to place her somewhere else. However, it is important to understand why the child was acting out and if anything occurred to precipitate the acting out behavior. Further, what else can be done to increase the level of services the child is receiving and to assess as many variables as possible before making a decision.
- Do not be afraid to disagree with someone. Critical thinking also involves evaluating positions of others and looking at all viewpoints. Many individuals readily agree with everyone but those who are truly utilizing critical thinking skills will disagree from time to time and provide rationale as to why they are seeing a different perspective. Disagreement may breed conflict from time to time but some conflict helps teams to focus more and challenge themselves.

Utilizing Problem Solving Skills

- One of the main points about effective problem solving for human service professionals is successfully working through barriers to meet client needs. There are a wide variety of unexpected client issues that can occur which require problem solving skills:
  - Lost placement/housing
  - Court dates being rescheduled
  - Courts not granting specific requests
  - Paperwork being misplaced
  - Parents not showing up for home visits/visitation with children
  - Client medical issues
- Effective problem solving entails
  - Understanding what the end product should be (i.e. knowing how the situation should work out and then working backwards to achieve the desired result).
    - Keith met his client, Jason, just before he was to be released from a juvenile program. Jason was not sure what he wanted but was

happy to be going home. Keith was concerned that without proper guidance and structure Jason would be at high risk to return to the same behaviors that led to his placement in a program. As such, he worked with Jason to develop a plan that would allow him to maximize his strengths and increase his academic skills. He started by asking Jason what he wanted to achieve after his release and from there they were able to come up with a plan to proactively work toward gaining employment and setting up tutoring to keep his academic performance in good standing.

- Arriving at a thoughtful decision on the best course of action (avoid making impulsive decisions without thinking them through).
- Anticipating obstacles and planning for them in case they arise.
- Teach clients the skills needed to work through potential issues on their own if they come up.
- Develop an action plan to help clients stay on track and achieve the goal(s) they are working toward.
- Other points about problem solving
  - Do not hesitate to draw upon the experiences of your coworkers and supervisor to help arrive at the best plan of action. Effective professionals consult with their colleagues-this helps to consider alternative points of view and to bounce ideas off of others who may have encountered the issue previously.
    - It is ok if you are unsure of the next steps to take when the process does not go as planned-utilize the assistance of coworkers and your supervisor but be sure to bring a proposed plan of action when presenting your situation (i.e. "I was thinking about trying....what are your thoughts about this approach?").

- Anticipate potential issues and have a backup plan just in case.
  - Brenda knew it was a possibility that Gina's parents would not show up for their scheduled visit due to missing the last two visits. As such, Gina was very anxious when she arrived for the visit due to the possibility that her parents would miss yet again. Brenda also knew it was likely so she phoned the foster home where Gina's brother was living to arrange a visit just in case the visit did not occur or did not go well as her brother was typically able to calm her down. When Gina's parents did not show up for the visit Brenda had a backup plan in place.

Going Above and Beyond

Maggie is the type of person that likes to ask questions and obtain as much information as possible. She does not like to work off assumptions and asks many questions so that she is fully informed. She recently received a client from another worker and wanted a detailed summary of why the agency was working with the client, presenting client issues, attempted interventions and outcomes, etc. While some of her peers joke that she is like a lawyer, Maggie wants to have as much information as possible.

Use critical thinking to optimize problem solving skills and professional credibility.

CHAPTER EIGHT

Peer Support

Effective professionals are able to utilize the help, expertise, and advice of their peers. Peer support goes both ways (giving and receiving) and it is important to be open to receiving help as well as being open to helping others. Research shows that professionals that have consistent peer support encounter much more success than those who do not. Whether you are a new or an experienced worker peer support is a vital part to keeping your stress level low and maximizing the organization's ability to help clients.

Examples of Peer Support
- Seeking out a colleague for feedback on how to handle a situation
  - Silvia was experiencing difficulty in working with a provider and asked one of her coworkers for guidance on how to approach them more efficiently. The coworker directed Silvia to a different person at the agency whom they have used and have had positive experiences with in the past. Silvia used this advice to greatly improve her outcomes and relationship with the provider.
- Asking for help
  - Judy had a home visit scheduled that she really needed to complete by the end of the month and she

just found out that one of her court hearings was also scheduled around the same time. Judy was able to have one of her coworkers cover the home visit so that she could attend the court hearing.

- Debriefing to maintain psychological health
  - Peer support is vital to maintain your psychological health. At times, secondary trauma can be a continuous factor for human service professionals and this can increase the likelihood of burnout. As such, it is critical to surround yourself with coworkers that can help to process the many emotions that can arise from working with clients and their difficult circumstances. Research shows that burnout is often tied to high levels of work stress and support from peers can reduce this problem.
    - Terry initiated an informal support group where she and several of her coworkers would meet for lunch once a month. Terry found the group very helpful as she learned a lot from her peers. She was also reassured that she was not the only one that struggled with specific issues.

Take an Active Role in Supporting Peers

- Take initiative
  - If you notice that one of your coworkers is struggling in an area do not hesitate to lend a hand. High performing teams are comprised of coworkers who look out for each other and do not hesitate to pitch in or lend their expertise.
  - Michelle overhead that Chris was having difficulty making placements with a specific provider. Michelle went to Chris to mention that she had a good relationship with the director of the agency and would be happy to make a call for her to help facilitate the placement referral for a client.
- Pay attention to what your coworkers are going through. Listen and keep your pulse on the activities of the depart-

ment so that you can be there to assist a coworker if needed.

Accept Peer Assistance

- It can be difficult to accept help from coworkers from time to time but effective professionals can put aside their ego to learn new skills and know that they do not have all of the answers.
- Even if you find yourself not in agreement with the help being offered, be grateful that someone is taking the time to help you. If coworkers see you as unappreciative of help it can quickly cause others to see you in a negative light.

Mentoring

- Research shows that those that have a mentor will enhance their career advancement, satisfaction, and earning power.
- Be a mentor.
  - New workers often struggle to learn how to navigate the organization and could benefit from someone taking the time to help them acclimate to their new surroundings.
    - Jenna takes initiative to help new workers learn about community providers and gives them a contact list to help expedite their knowledge. She also checks in with new workers to see if they have any questions and will pass along tips that help her as well.
- Seek out a mentor.
  - Many organizations do not have a formal mentoring program so it is up to the employee to seek out a suitable mentor. This can be a difficult process as some senior workers are not interested in this function, however it does not have to be a formal relationship with set meetings. Instead, it can be informal meetings periodically designed to help the worker learn valuable insights from the experienced professional.

- Take initiative to surround yourself with individuals that will enhance your knowledge and performance.

Going Above and Beyond

When Tina first started with the agency she struggled with her position, the responsibilities, and the policies/procedures. She sought out a seasoned worker to see if she could help be a guide and she was glad that Lucy accepted. Tina and Lucy meet for lunch every week and this serves as an opportunity for Tina to ask questions and obtain guidance from a senior worker that she trusts and admires. Lucy also likes mentoring others.

**Seek out and initiate peer support
to improve service delivery
and psychological health.**

CHAPTER NINE
Cultural Competence

One of the keys to effectively engaging clients is to be mindful of their cultural background and how that impacts their worldview and subsequent behavior. Communities are becoming more diverse and human service organizations have a duty to meet the needs of the residents that they serve. As such, professionals need to be knowledgeable about the cultural background of their clients.

Culture has many different meanings but generally has to do with a shared pattern of beliefs, behaviors and viewpoints by a specific group of people. Effective human service professionals do not need to be experts about the cultural backgrounds of all clients but should have a basic understanding of the cultures of their clients.

Cultural Competency Means
- Knowing the cultural backgrounds of your clients. Culture cannot be ignored and plays a pivotal role in creating effective interventions that will help the client/family. Take time during the intake process and/or during initial meetings with your client to learn about them and the role of their culture in shaping their behavior and viewpoints.
    - Do your research to find out about your client's culture and subculture. Consider internet searches as well as collaborating with coworkers who have personal knowledge about a specific culture to find out more information.

- Asking questions. Make an effort to learn as much as you can about the client's cultural background. Asking questions demonstrates to your clients a willingness to learn about them and their culture, which enhances rapport and relationship building.
- Not making assumptions. Even if a client appears to be of a certain ethnicity or culture do not assume.
  - For example, an individual may appear to be Hispanic due to their skin color and/or their last name but be mindful to not assume this. Further, even if an individual does come from a Hispanic background it cannot be assumed that they speak Spanish.
- Challenging assumptions. Many of us possess preconceived notions of specific groups due to messages from friends, family, and coworkers throughout our lives but be mindful to learn about the cultures and make your own decisions.
- Knowing the demographics of your community. Effective human service professionals are knowledgeable about the cultural diversity in their community as well as trends that can impact service delivery.
- Understanding how culture influences behavior. What may be a common approach to one may not be to another. Take into consideration what is the client's culture when working with them.
  - Jennifer was working with a family where the house was dirty and she would see roaches from time to time. She did not grow up in a house like that coming from a middle class background and instantly thought the children were in danger due to the unclean environment. However, after discussing the case with her supervisor she gained more insight of the family's culture and realized that she was not in a position to force her culture upon any client. She was there to help them maximize their skills to the best of their ability.
- Utilizing resources to expand your knowledge of dominant cultures in your area. Seek out books and credible online resources like Georgetown University's National Center for Cultural Competence at www.nccc.georgetown.edu

Going Above and Beyond

Milena is widely recognized throughout her agency as having a skill for connecting with clients of all different backgrounds. One of the keys to her success is knowing about the culture of the client that she is working with. Milena identifies herself as a Caucasian woman, which does not interfere with her ability to work with clients from a variety of different backgrounds. She makes it a point to research about the client's culture and will ask her colleagues if she is unsure of how to approach a specific situation. She also keeps a calendar with different cultural holidays so that she can keep abreast of upcoming cultural/religious celebrations.

**Effective human service professionals
are very knowledgeable about
the cultural backgrounds of their clients.**

CHAPTER TEN

Professionalism

Professional behavior is what provides the human service worker with the highest credibility. The definition of professional behavior may vary for some, but it generally focuses on character, integrity, and pride. Take pride in presenting with the highest level of professionalism across all situations, as this will greatly enhance your reputation with clients and with the organization.

Professional Behavior Defined

- Stay true to your word. Whether you are following up for a client or someone within your agency it is essential to deliver on commitments. If you are not able to complete a task within a specific timeframe inform the party of the barrier/challenge that you encountered and give them a new timeframe for when they can expect for the task to be completed.
  - Kerry's clients always know that when she sets an appointment with them that she will be on time. If she is running late she will call and inform them of when to expect her.
  - Janet attended a treatment team meeting for one of her clients and she committed to completing an assessment referral for them before she left on vacation. Although she had other tasks to complete before going out, she worked late that week to ensure that all commitments were kept before she left for vacation.

- Deliver on time, or preferably be early. Professionals can quickly earn a positive reputation by completing assignments on time and early. However, ensure that the quality of your work is not impacted by completing work early.
- Return phone calls and emails in a timely manner. In some instances it may be up to 24 hours before you return a call or email but make every effort to do so within a few hours, if possible. Demonstrating to clients and other professionals that you respond in a timely manner is a skill that stands out.
- Keep all parties informed. Informing is a key competency to possess. Be careful to not over-inform others as too much information becomes unnecessary.
- Be mindful about your actions/behavior. Human service professionals are aware to demonstrate the most professional behavior at all times. Professional action/behavior means:
  - Avoid gossiping. Some coworkers in your agency may actively engage in this but minimize how much participation you have in those conversations. In many cases it is best to walk away. Gossip about other employees can be damaging, destructive, and counterproductive. Also, if you are associated with those that gossip it can have a negative impact on your reputation within the agency.
  - Reframing issues into a strength based approach. It can be easy to see the negative in situations (i.e. client behavior, constant changes in the organization, complaints about the supervisor, etc.) but professional behavior means not speaking down about others and looking for the positives. If you cannot find anything positive to say refrain from making any comments.
  - Do not allow yourself to become overly frustrated. There will be times in which you may not receive the outcome that you were intending but do not allow for your frustrations to be observed by others or impact your ability to perform your job duties. It

is usually best to allow time to pass before approaching the situation so that emotions do not become involved.

- Justin received information from another provider that his client failed their drug test, meaning that all of the efforts he put in place for overnight visitation would not occur. He was highly frustrated about the outcome but waited until later in the day to speak with his client to find out how the positive test occurred rather than calling the client as soon as he found out the results.

- Use diplomacy. Effective professionals are able to focus on the needs of the client, not their ego, regardless of the actions of others. You will encounter other professionals who demonstrate behavior that may not be considered professional but do not allow that to impact your approach.
  - Compliment when others do well.
  - Be polite-say please and thank you often.
  - Avoid making the other person lose face or look bad-relationships are important.
  - Give others the benefit of the doubt even if you do not agree with their position.
  - Ask questions to understand why the other party believes in their position.
  - Use facts to support your position.
  - Embrace conflict-disagreements can help you to grow and consider alternative positions to enhance client care.

- Dress in a professional manner: Whether attending meetings or court hearings be sure you wear the appropriate attire. Professionals that dress well for specific occasions (i.e. meetings) stand out within their agency and the community. Take pride in your everyday attire and ensure that it communicates a highly professional image. Utilize the approach of being the best dressed employee in the office/agency, when possible.

- Be prepared: When attending meetings be sure you have done your homework and are up to date on all relevant issues of the case before entering the meeting. A worker will lose credibility if they show up lacking sufficient knowledge about the client. It is recommended that you review your notes and bring the case file to meetings so that you can quickly reference information for the team to review.
  - Kelly had a meeting to discuss a child's behavior in the classroom and why an alternative placement would be in his best interest. She typed up information to demonstrate how often he had been suspended over the prior three months in addition to specific classroom behaviors. She used facts and was well versed in the child's behaviors to inform the team members.

Going Above and Beyond

Mary makes it a point to always dress well and to stand out as a professional. She likes to dress a little better than her peers because her appearance is important to her as well as how she presents to clients and in the community. Further, she makes it a point to provide thoughtful responses to clients and other professionals and to always remain calm regardless of the situation. Mary's professional behavior has led to several job offers over the years, often for positions that she did not apply for.

Highly professional behavior is directly related to your professional reputation and credibility.

CHAPTER ELEVEN

Be a Resource Expert

Clients seek assistance for a variety of reasons. Often, their main presenting issue may lead to them needing help in other areas. This is why human service professionals need to be highly knowledgeable about resources on a variety of levels so that they can be a valuable advocate for their clients. Clients rely on workers to have knowledge about a wide variety of resources in the community.

Being a Resource Expert Involves

- Possessing advanced knowledge of programs and services within your community.
    - It is vital to know all of the providers that you work with as well as the specific services that they provide.
        - Be sure to thoroughly know the services that are provided. Clients rely on professionals to have a firm grasp of what is available.
    - You should also have contact information (email, fax, office/cell phone, etc.) for each provider.
    - If you do not know about the specific services that are provided find out and get back to the individual as soon as possible.
- Having an excellent relationship with providers.
    - Use your relationship building skills to keep in consistent contact with key people at the agencies that you regularly work with. This will help to keep you

abreast of any changes (i.e. staff and/or programs) that occur.
- Knowing about programs outside of your area.
  - Be knowledgeable about programs that are not within your scope of services but you may be asked about.
    - Susan is a foster care worker that completes home studies on potential foster parents. One of her parents needed help in seeking counseling for her child and Susan was able to quickly consult with her coworkers as well as complete an internet search of providers in the area that could be contacted.
- Developing an essential resource guide for you and your coworkers.
  - The guide should contain vital information such as
    - Name
    - Address
    - Phone (office and cell phone)
    - Fax
    - Services provided
    - Thorough description of programs and services
    - Key contacts
- Keeping a quick reference guide with you that contains easy to access information about each provider that is 1-2 pages in length. This will allow you to always have information at your fingertips regardless of the situation.

Going Above and Beyond

Bertha is a family service specialist for a Head Start program. She often has to access a wide variety of community resources to help the families that she works with. Bertha is typically able to steer her families in the right direction due to the vast knowledge that she has about community resources. She has accumulated a great deal of knowledge throughout her time working at the agency through meetings attended and regular contact with surrounding agencies.

Stand out with advanced knowledge of community programs and resources.

CHAPTER TWELVE

Work/Life Balance

Working in the human services can be a rewarding yet stressful occupation. Moreover, individuals who choose to work in the field do so because of their desire to help others, but sometimes they can give too much. This is why having a balance between your work and personal life is essential in maintaining a high level of performance over the long-term. Human service professionals that do not make it a priority to make time for their personal lives greatly increase the likelihood of burnout and reduced effectiveness, which is a great concern in certain sectors of the field. Remain mindful of the potential impacts of burnout, emotional exhaustion, and secondary trauma.

Common Factors that May Increase Stress

- High caseloads
- Hostile clients
- Lack of community resources to meet client needs
- Changes in policies and procedures and/or staff
- Inadequate/ineffective supervision
- Lack of supervisor/agency support
- High profile/difficult cases
- Low pay
- Getting behind in work (especially after coming back from time off)
- Criticism from supervisor, parents, or coworkers
- Not feeling as though you are able to make a difference

Indicators of Stress

- Physical
  - Decrease in appetite, sleep and/or personal appearance
  - Poor concentration
  - Headaches and body pains
- Behavioral
  - Arguing with others
  - Difficulty maintaining conversations with others
  - Increase in time off
  - Spending increased amount of time at work but not being as productive
  - Withdrawing from others
- Emotional
  - Difficulty in making decisions
  - Feeling anxious and/or nervous
  - Depressed
  - Irritability/short fuse
  - Lack of humor

Strategies to Achieve Work/Life Balance

- Understand that the job will sometimes, depending on the type of organization that you work for, require more than 40 hours a week and work around it.
  - Diane routinely sets aside two days a week where she works later to complete her home visits. She is able to plan her schedule around these times. Her family also understands that she will be home toward the evening during those days.
    - Schedule as many visits at the beginning of the month as possible to allow for ample time to address unplanned issues that may arise.
- Working in the human services often requires professionals to give a lot of themselves. It is important to understand your limitations and to set up boundaries that will allow you to achieve a proper balance.

- Catherine often worked into the evenings several days a week and this was impacting her personal life. She realized one day that she was no longer able to give so much at her job due to the consequences that it was having on her personal life and made it a point to only work late one day a week. This allowed her to have the time needed for her personal life in addition to being more focused on her work.
- The human services field has rapidly evolved into one that frequently uses technology to increase response times (i.e. use of email and smart phone technology). This can place increased stress on workers who feel the constant need to answer phone calls and emails after the workday has ended.
  - Be mindful that not every phone call and email is a priority that needs to be responded to. In fact, many after hour phone calls and emails can be replied to the next day-this can reduce a great deal of stress and allow you to enjoy your time away from work.
- Schedule time off. Even if it is one day during the month on a Friday or Monday. Having an extra day off can provide needed time to recharge and refocus. Sometimes individuals may be reluctant to schedule time off due to the large amount of work that may be waiting for them upon their return but it is necessary.
  - Professionals who do not take ample time are at an increased risk for burnout and emotional exhaustion.
- Prioritize.
  - If you look at everything that needs to be done it can be easy to become overwhelmed. Group your tasks into priority level (i.e. urgent to not urgent), make a list, and complete one by one.
- Enjoy hobbies.
  - Take time to develop interests outside of work. Well-rounded individuals are better advocates for their clients. Do not let work be your life, enjoy things outside of work and allow yourself to disconnect and not check email and voicemail when you are not at work.

- Ask for help.
  - If there is a point when the stress of the job are becoming too much and other interventions have not helped do not hesitate to ask for help from your supervisor. It is better to proactively ask for help from your supervisor before your work performance gets to the point where they have to use disciplinary action.
  - There are also times where it may be better to seek a transfer to another department/position if the stress of the work is too much. Again, there may be other ways that you can still impact clients but in a position that works better for you and the agency-speak to your supervisor and/or your human resources department if this is a consideration.
- Use humor.
  - Research has shown that individuals who use humor are better able to cope with the stress that comes from working in the human services. Take time to laugh throughout the day. Understand that some humor may only be shared with coworkers to take the edge of off serious situations.
- Maintain empathy.
  - Regardless of the stress that you encounter, always remember to meet every client where they are that and take effort to see where they are coming from. Empathy is a core competency for working in the human services.
- Self-awareness is vital.
  - Be mindful of your emotional and physical state and how that impacts your personal and professional performance/relationships. If you find yourself becoming overwhelmed, acknowledge this feeling and seek solutions (i.e. time off, speak to your peers or supervisor about strategies to assist, etc.)
- Be optimistic.
  - Change can happen, even in the unlikeliest of circumstances. There are times when the human service

professional is the last person in the client's life who believes in their ability to change. The client may change after your contact with them and sometimes it is important to take solace in knowing that our efforts may help them in the future.

- Use of peer support.
  - Peer support is an essential part of effectively managing work stress. Due to the complex nature of the work it is important to have a peer group that you can bounce ideas off as well as receive support when you are encountering a difficult situation. Many individuals find their peer support groups so valuable it is an important factor in whether they remain with the organization.
- Self-care is at the heart of effectively managing stress and maintaining a proper work/life balance.
  - Working out and exercising
  - Eating healthy meals, even while at work
  - Getting enough sleep
  - Enjoying the company of friends and family
  - Providing yourself with small rewards throughout the week/month/and year to reinforce your hard work.
- Professional satisfaction and creating meaning.
  - Burnout effects are minimized when you have a job that you enjoy and consistently create opportunities to feel fulfilled.
- Continue to learn.
  - Learning is an ongoing process, both personally and professionally. Learning expands your perspective and opens up opportunities for development and growth. A "yearning burning for learning" as one manager stated.

Going Above and Beyond

Chris has been a re-entry counselor with a juvenile probation organization for several years. While there have been times that he has had a high caseload he has been able to manage the stress of the job by making use of his time off. He will occasionally take off a Friday and Monday so that he has a long weekend and will use his vacation time to take a week long cruise in the summers. Chris really enjoys working with youth but also realizes that he needs time for himself to be at his best, both personally and professionally.

A work/life balance will enhance your ability to assist clients and professional fulfillment.

CHAPTER THIRTEEN

Maintaining Your Passion

Burnout, stress, and emotional exhaustion are occupational hazards of working in the human services. Professionals sometimes lose sight of why they originally entered the field and this has a tremendous impact on their approach toward clients. Above all, it is essential to maintain your passion for helping others and create opportunities, regardless of your position and job duties, that will allow you to enjoy working in the field.

How to Maintain Your Passion for Helping Others

- Do not lose sight of why you entered the human services. It is understood that most of us did not enter the field for the prospect of making large sums of money. As such, take a moment to periodically reflect at what brought you into the field-it may have been a desire at an early age to help others, personal experience, etc. Nevertheless, maintain a connection with the initial reason that drew you into the helping profession.
- Research points out that many professionals leave the human services due to feeling that they are not making enough of an impact for their clients. This is a reality that many feel and administrative and/or agency constraints can add to the "red tape" that creates barriers to effectively helping clients in need.
    - Effective professionals understand the limitations that are in place and that they are not able to help

every client in the way that they feel is best. It is important to consider that there is limited funding and resources available and not every client may qualify for the services that they appear to need or could benefit from receiving.

- Create opportunities to engage clients in a meaningful way. Regardless of your position and how much contact you have with clients, take advantage of chances that may arise throughout the day or week where you can engage clients. This may be through volunteering to answer phones, cover the front desk, etc.
- Find resources that will ignite your passion for helping others and making a difference. Sometimes a movie, television show, or book may leave you feeling compelled to make a difference-use this to help re-energize you.
- Working in the human services should be more than a paycheck. Clients deserve professionals who are friendly, courteous, and willing to go above and beyond to help them. If you find that it is difficult for you to engage clients in this manner you may want to consider re-evaluating your perspective and take a step back to see where you can change.
- Personal flexibility is critical. Some professionals develop a rigid outlook regarding clients and this negatively impacts the professional as well as having an impact on their approach to helping others. Remain mindful that everyone has a personal story as to why they are seeking services (i.e. job loss, insurance does not cover services needed for a child, etc.).
- Find other ways to contribute to the community. Consider volunteering from time to time to help others in ways that you may have become removed from. Many professionals who have taken on other positions or have seen their job duties change miss the interaction with clients and helping to solve client problems.
- Be present. Regardless of the activity that you are engaging in be fully present in the moment. Even though you may have completed a task many times it does not mean that the client is aware of the process. Stop and take time to ensure

that you are explaining the process so that they can understand.

- Make small talk with the client. This can help to build rapport as well as keep you engaged.
- Utilize peer support. Speak to coworkers about challenges that they face and how they maintain their passion for helping others. Sometimes a colleague may have an interesting perspective that may be useful.
- Keep reminders in your office. Use quotes or other mementos to help keep you focused on the value of helping others. If you receive thank you cards from clients keep them available to help keep you motivated.
- Understand that everything that you do, even though it may not provide immediate results, has an impact on clients. Some work is behind the scenes and helps to benefit others.

Going Above and Beyond

Martha has been working for a developmental disability organization for 15 years. She has had a few positions with the agency during that time but has mostly been in a case management role. Even though much of her tasks are routine she still gets excited whenever she is able to make a difference with her clients. She takes advantage of any opportunity to use her problem solving abilities to make a difference for her client and/or their families. She loves challenges and seeing how happy her clients are when she is able to help.

Never forget why you chose to work in the human services-that will keep your passion for helping strong.

CHAPTER FOURTEEN

Forming and Maintaining a Positive Supervisor Relationship

Having a positive and productive relationship with your supervisor is a key component of effectively navigating the terrain of the human services. The role of the supervisor is to guide, model, and support you in your growth as a professional. The role of the worker is just as important to ensuring the relationship is a positive one so take an active role in forming and maintaining a strong partnership.

Forming and Maintaining a Positive Supervisor Relationship Involves

- Taking initiative.
    - Every supervisor loves a worker who will take initiative to help others and take the lead with new projects. Depending on your work schedule take the lead with a new project.
- Delivering on time and following through.
    - Be sure that all projects, reports, etc. are completed on time, early if possible, so that your supervisor can have enough time to review your work and provide feedback.
- Offering suggestions and ideas.
    - There will be situations where a coworker or the team struggles to find a solution. Do not be afraid to offer a suggestion or a potential solution that the

59

team can consider. This is an excellent way to help the supervisor so that they are not the only ones offering up ideas.

• Being loyal.
  • While rarely discussed every supervisor wants their staff to be loyal to them. Staff loyalty involves looking out for your supervisor and if others are speaking negatively about them to not allow the conversation to go further. Think of how you would want your staff to treat you behind your back if you were a supervisor.

• Being positive.
  • There will be a variety of challenges to remaining positive but this is a critical part of being an effective human service professional. Whether it is adding more work or changing systems it is vital to remain positive at all times. Being positive means remaining upbeat and looking for the good in a situation regardless of how it may impact you. Supervisors appreciate staff that can remain positive even in the most challenging of situations.

• Being proactive in asking for help.
  • Sometimes we like to work on an issue ourselves rather than asking for help. However, it is good practice to seek supervisor assistance before the issue impacts the way others see your performance and ability to help clients. If initial efforts to solve the issue by yourself are not successful, do not hesitate to ask your supervisor for assistance, especially during high profile cases.

• Defining what support looks like for you.
  • Support is a general term that looks different for everyone. As such, take time to define what support means to you (i.e. kudos when you are doing well, guidance on difficult cases, access to resources, listening to your frustrations without judgment, etc.).

- Regularly asking for feedback.
  - An important part of being an effective professional is asking for feedback on your performance. Some agencies have a formal process where the supervisor conducts a monthly supervision meeting to discuss cases and provide feedback and some do not. Either way, take initiative to ask your supervisor for feedback on your performance. Be consistent with asking for it regardless of the response that you get. Professionals that are serious about their growth regularly ask for feedback.
- Being open to feedback.
  - Whether the feedback is provided because you ask for it or not it is important to not be defensive when feedback is provided. Sometimes we may not agree with the feedback that is provided but this can provide an opportunity to reflect on our performance and assess why someone may make a particular observation.
    - Elaine was provided feedback from her supervisor about an observation that she made from a recent interaction Elaine had with a client. Elaine's supervisor remarked that Elaine appeared to be too emotionally involved with the situation and encouraged her to reflect on her ability to remain objective to client needs. While Elaine did not agree with the feedback at first, she put much thought into the feedback and agreed with the assessment and spoke to her supervisor the next day and asked for feedback on how to correct her behavior.
- Openly discussing issues and providing feedback
  - Communication that goes both ways is an essential part of making any relationship work. The same goes for the work-supervisor relationship. While it is expected that most of the communication may come from your supervisor it is important to keep

them informed of issues so that they do not have to routinely ask you. Make it a habit to proactively provide information to your supervisor so that they are not underinformed of issues.

- It is also important to know that you can provide feedback to your supervisor. Feedback does not only go one way and it is empowering to know that you can provide them with feedback as well. Providing feedback to your supervisor should be handled with care to ensure that you are being professional at all times. It is good for the worker to know that if something is bothering them about the relationship they can freely share it, as long as they remain professional.

  - Jesse was upset with a decision that his supervisor made to reverse a decision that he made about a client being denied for benefits. He asked to speak to his supervisor when they had a moment and professionally asked why the decision was made (i.e. "May I ask why the Taylor family's benefits were reinstated?"). After the explanation was provided Jesse then stated that he would appreciate if the supervisor would inform him directly if one of his decisions were overturned rather than hearing from someone else. The supervisor agreed with his request and advised that she would keep him informed of any future concerns.

    - Open communication minimizes resentment from either party and allows for the processing of emotions and clarification of concerns. This is why it is important to discuss issues before it impacts work performance.

- Being prepared.

  - Preparation demonstrates commitment and professional behavior to your supervisor. Be sure to be prepared for supervision meetings by having all case related information ready ahead of time. After time you should be able to anticipate the questions and information that your supervisor needs-do your homework before the meeting so that this information is readily available. If you are unsure of the common types of information that your supervisor needs during specific meetings, ask.

- It is also important to always have a good understanding of your clients so that if your supervisor asks about a case you can provide them with the information that they need. Ensure your files are up to date so that they can access them and be able to know the progress of a case without having to speak with you. There are times when upper management may have a question for them on a case so it is important to keep your files in good condition at all times.
- Taking ownership.
    - Effective human service professionals take ownership of their behaviors and choices. If your supervisors asks why a decision was made, provide the reasoning and rationale. If your supervisor does not agree with it ask for feedback of what could have been done differently. Feedback is an opportunity to learn.
    - Take responsibility for your clients and demonstrate pride in the progress that they make.
- Making your supervisor look good.
    - It is a reciprocal relationship so looking out for your supervisor is always in your best interest.

Avoid Being a Difficult Employee

- Managers often struggle with employees that are difficult and this can lead to them spending a great deal of time on one employee rather than focusing on department issues and improving client care. Common issues that supervisors have to deal with include, but are not limited to the following employee behaviors:

- Defensive/not taking accountability
- Negative
- Oppositional and/or challenging authority
- Emotional reaction to feedback
- Blaming others
- Not a team player
- Passive aggressive
- Lack of motivation to do more than the bare minimum
- Remain mindful of these behaviors and reflect on your performance to ensure that your behavior does not fall into these categories.

Going Above and Beyond

Marti is considered to be a highly valued employee in her department. She remains positive even during highly stressful times and can be counted on to speak up during staff meetings. While her ideas are not always implemented she is not afraid to give her feedback and ask questions. Additionally, her supervisor appreciates how Marti keeps her informed and for the high level of preparation that she undertakes for all meetings.

Form a partnership with your supervisor to help guide your growth and development.

CHAPTER FIFTEEN

Drive for Improvement and Growth

A sign of a highly effective professional is their commitment for improvement. Few workers start a position with a high level of information and ability to perform the job without guidance and this is why commitment toward personal growth is important. Effective human service professionals take advantage of any opportunity to learn new skills and information that will help them excel in their ability to meet client needs.

Maximizing Professional Growth

- Always remain mindful that human service professionals encourage clients to grow so it is important to utilize this approach for yourself.
- Regardless of how long you have been in the field or your current job it is vital to actively seek out trainings that will challenge you and aide in your growth and development. With the rapid evolution of technology it is vital to remain ahead of the trend so that you can continue to meet client needs.
- Help your organization's view of growth and development by offering solutions and suggesting trainings that could benefit your coworkers. Do not hesitate to suggest trainings because as a direct line worker you have the best perspective of the needs of you and your coworkers.

- Actively seek out trainings that will add to your growth and development. Find out agencies that provide trainings in your community (some do it for free or at low cost) and regularly review their training calendar to find a training that fits for you.
- Read books, magazines, and online articles that will expand your knowledge in specific areas of interest. Sometimes your organization will subscribe to resources which would be helpful to read.
  - Read information from other sources not related to the human services. It is important to have a well-rounded view and this can be accomplished by gaining knowledge from as many different areas as possible. Well-rounded professionals have more to offer clients.
- Constantly evaluate your approach and performance to find areas of improvement. Effective professionals are continuously looking at their performance and seeking opportunities for improvement. Ask for feedback from others and be appreciative of any insight and perspective that is offered. All forms of feedback help us grow.
- See what approaches work for your coworkers. If there is a certain approach that a coworker uses to work with resistant clients incorporate it into your repertoire. Be open to sharing your approaches that work so that information can be freely shared.
- Above all, be assertive with your professional growth and encourage your supervisor and organization to look into trainings that can help you and your coworkers grow and develop. However, with tight budgets training dollars are usually difficult to come by. This is why it is vital for you to take ownership of your growth by continually seeking out opportunities within the community or on your own to meet your professional needs.

Going Above and Beyond

Toni was excited when her organization purchased an e-learning program. The program offered a wide variety of trainings that enabled her to complete trainings in areas that challenged her. While she is required to complete 40 hours a training each year she would consistently complete much more than required due to her desire to learn as much as possible, even on areas that were outside of her current responsibilities. Toni also likes to visit websites on a monthly basis that cover topics in her field so that she can stay updated on trends impacting clients.

Effective professionals maintain a strong desire for continuous personal growth and development.

CHAPTER SIXTEEN

Actively Contribute to Your Organization

The role of an effective human service professional extends beyond high quality client care. Professionals are expected to be active contributors to the culture of the agency. Organizations need individuals to take the lead in participating in functions, large and small, to help create a culture that is fun, challenging, and stimulating.

How to Contribute to Your Agency

- Take ownership and have pride in the organization for which you work. We spend the majority of our time at work-take an active role in helping to make the agency one that people look forward to coming to work every day.
- Ask yourself "what can I do to make the agency better?"
  - It starts with wanting to do more than the bare minimum. Effective human service professionals possess a natural desire to help others and the agency is an extension of this. The agency is more than a building with walls and offices-it houses individuals who want to help as many people as possible.
- Believe in the agency mission and cause to help others.
  - With the high demands that are sometimes placed on workers it can be easy to forget why you and the agency are there. Be sure to align your work and efforts with the agency mission.

- Be active in meetings.
  - Resist the temptation not participate in meetings for feeling that your ideas will be disregarded. Regardless of the meeting you are attending (client related, department, etc.) be active, engaged, and participate with questions and potential solutions.
- Create opportunities to participate in projects that have meaning for you.
  - Anthony has experience working with human trafficking at a previous position and he offered to participate in a program on human trafficking that met monthly. He would share the learned information with his colleagues and supervisor and would provide the material to be included in the agency's monthly newsletter.
- Be a cheerleader.
  - Encourage your coworkers to go above and beyond. Provide praise for colleagues who help others and share the praise so that as many people take initiative as possible.
- Participate in committees.
  - Some organizations have committees designed to improve employee retention, organizational performance, etc. Find out about existing committees and see if you can participate, depending on your schedule and ability to complete your job duties.
  - Make suggestions for committees. Committees are an excellent way for professionals to get together with a goal of improving the agency. Consider speaking with your supervisor and other colleagues to see if they would be interested in forming and participating in a committee that can benefit the agency (employee appreciation, cultural competence, ways to improve service delivery for clients, etc.).
- Volunteer.
  - Many agencies participate in activities to raise money or awareness for specific issues. Be part of

the activities as your schedule allows as this shows your support for initiatives that will benefit the community and the clients that you serve.
- Take initiative to help others.
  - Departments may be understaffed and sometimes need help so that the existing workers do not become overwhelmed. See how you can help in small ways like answering phones for one hour a week or staying late one night every few weeks to help file.
- Demonstrate every day leadership.
  - Leadership is for everyone regardless of their position in the agency. Do not hesitate to offer ideas that will enhance the client experience with the agency as well as ways to enhance organizational processes.
- Do not hesitate to help but be mindful of your time and job duties.
  - It is great to help others but always be sure that you are able to complete your own tasks as well as have time for yourself. If you overextend yourself you will not be effective in any area.
- You have the ability to help transform your department and agency into one that is full of energy and pride.

Going Above and Beyond

Nathan enjoys working for his present organization. He has been there five years and still feels happy coming to work in the morning. He takes the opportunity to volunteer for different committees and has been recognized for having ideas that has helped improve service delivery for clients. He was recently recognized for helping another department to complete home visits until a new person was hired and oriented.

Choose to bring energy and enthusiasm to help build a productive department/agency.

CHAPTER SEVENTEEN

High Quality Work Performance

There is an ongoing challenge for human service professionals to deliver a high quality work product while meeting client needs with limited resources. Still, it is imperative that workers continually strive to provide the highest quality performance in all domains. Clients deserve the best regardless of the situation.

How to Achieve High Quality

- Attention to detail.
    - Read reports over carefully to ensure they contain the right names and other important information. There are times when information may be cut and pasted into multiple reports and this can reduce the credibility of the professional.
    - Ensure spelling and grammar is correct.
    - Read over your work at least twice to ensure that it flows and contains all necessary information
- Take your time.
    - There are few occasions in the human services that require an immediate response. As such, take time to complete tasks with a high degree of quality. Budget enough time to allow for quality completion of important tasks (i.e. court reports).
- Utilize examples and guides.
    - Find example reports or locate a report completed by a peer that is regarded as having strength in the

area. Keep example reports around to provide guidance on areas to cover, phrases to use, flow of information, etc.

- Ryan was a new case manager and sought out a peer for guidance in completing a court report. He was able to gain reports from different colleagues and redacted all identifying information so that he could keep them. He was able to learn how to write in a concise and objective manner so that his reports were also considered to be high quality.

- Find resources.
  - A book like *The Clinician's Thesaurus* is an example of a resource that can provide ample examples of how to write in a more clinical and professional manner. Find websites, journal articles, and books that can provide reference materials to help enhance your knowledge and writing ability.
- Seek out trainings.
  - Sometimes struggles may be associated with a lack of knowledge. Work with your supervisor to identify trainings provided by the agency or seek outside trainings to expand your skillset.
- Ask for feedback.
  - Ask your supervisor for regular feedback on your work performance and recommendations for how you can improve in specific areas. Do not be afraid to ask for peer feedback as well as recommendations for improvement.
- Be critical of your work.
  - In order to consistently produce high quality work, being self-critical is an important factor. Being critical means reviewing your work carefully and not hesitating to start over or go in a different direction if needed.

Going Above and Beyond

Samantha takes pride in her work and the reputation that she has earned within the organization and the community. She takes extra time when needed to ensure that the work that she completes is of high quality. Samantha rarely needs to add information to her reports due to how thorough they are. She has several books in her office that she uses to give her guidance on how to write reports that are of excellent quality. Many coworkers frequently ask Samantha for advice because of her high quality work.

Take pride in consistently delivering high quality performance.

CHAPTER EIGHTEEN

Excellent Customer Service

High quality customer service skills are expected at all times within the human services. It can be challenging when you have to interact with difficult clients or other professionals but it is important to set and maintain the standard for what positive customer service looks like across all situations. Professionals that are calm and pleasant tend to be more effective.

Defining Excellent Customer Service Skills

- Consider where the individual is coming from.
  - Clients experience a variety of barriers and challenges to effectively accessing services. They may also lack the ability to navigate through these barriers and this can add to the frustration that they are already experiencing. It is important to be mindful of what your clients may be going through and use empathy to try and place yourself in their situation. Imagine what it must be like to lose custody of your children.
- Clarify the position.
  - Sometimes clients may complain for so long or be so upset they may lose sight of the source of their frustration. Ask open ended questions to find out what their experience has been. Examples include: "Can you tell me how long that has been occurring?" "When did you call?" "Who did you speak with?"

- Validate the person and the challenges they are facing.
    - Sometimes individuals feel as though no one is listening to them or attempting to understand their situation. Phrases such as, "It sounds like you have a lot going on right now." or "I would be frustrated if that happened to me, too." Validating can be a useful tool to calm down an angry client.
- Active listening
    - Demonstrate that you are paying attention. Depending on the client or their behavior it may be challenging to remain focused and present but avoid the temptation of losing focus. Restate their positions and remain involved in the conversation. You typically do not need to talk much when clients are venting-ask questions and be present.
- Be patient.
    - As long as the client is not becoming rude and using profanity allow the client to vent. Sometimes that can be therapeutic for them to vent their frustrations but remain focused on the actual complaint and potential solutions.
- Do not take client behavior personally.
    - More often than not client frustration is blamed at the system and not one person. However, the individual who is working with the client may take the brunt of client misbehavior. Either way, do not take their actions personally even if
- Be pleasant and smile.
    - Stay one step ahead of clients by beginning any conversation with a pleasant and cheerful tone. The positive energy of the professional can make a big difference with the quality of engagement with clients regardless of the situation.
- The customer is not always right.
    - There are many times in which the client is not correct. In fact, they may have made an error and are not taking ownership for their behavior. For example, a client may have missed a deadline to submit a

housing application and lost out on the opportunity for section 8 housing. The client may then become upset with the worker or the agency for making them miss the deadline. Still, it is important to be professional even if the client did make a mistake. It is not about proving that the client was wrong.

- Be professional at all times.
  - Regardless of how the client is behavior do not allow yourself to enter a situation where your behavior deteriorates. Maintain appropriate and professional behavior (i.e. do not resort to using profanity or raising your voice). If the client becomes rude and disrespectful, end the conversation.
    - Nora was having a conversation with a client who was upset with how her son was being treated in the group home. Donald was not able to go on a visit with his mom due to having an aggressive episode the day before his visit. The mother wanted the visit to occur anyway and after a few minutes she began to use profanity and insult Nora. Nora remained calm during the situation and professionally informed the mother that if she continued to raise her voice and use profanity the conversation would end. The mother continued to behave in an irate manner and Nora ended the phone call with, "Ms. Smith I am sorry but that language is not acceptable. I am going to be hanging up the phone. Feel free to call me back after you calm down and we can discuss how to arrange Donald's visit for next weekend."
- Take ownership when necessary.
  - If you have made a mistake apologize and take responsibility. That can make the conversation much more pleasant and shorter if you are able to own up to your mistakes. Also, this helps to model

the same behavior to the client and provide an opportunity to address their behavior in the future if they make a mistake.

* Follow through.
    * If you make a commitment to a client be sure to keep it in the timeframe that you stated. This is an important component to excellent customer service skills. Clients want to see a resolution to their issue(s).

Excellent Customer Service Skills with Internal and External Professionals

* High quality customer service skills are not only reserved for clients, they are also used with members of your organization and other professionals. The same skills as mentioned above apply to internal and external professionals. It is important to remember how professionals need to work together and utilize a high level of professionalism with each other at all times.
* Main points of customer service with internal and external professionals include:
    * Take the opportunity to help out when needed. Pay it forward.
    * Remain focused on the client's best interest and avoid negativity.
    * Avoid personal feelings with coworkers. There may be some coworkers that you do not get along with or do not agree with their behavior but put this aside when working together so it does not delay the process.
    * Be sure to follow through in a timely manner.
* Be pleasant, professional, and respectful at all times.

Going Above and Beyond

Angela is an effective case manager who works closely with clients. She does hold her clients accountable and some have difficulty accepting ownership of their behavior and choices. She makes it a habit to greet clients warmly and establish a genuine relationship with them so it is easier to have difficult conversations with them. However, from time to time some clients will become rude and disrespectful toward Angela and she is patient, yet firm regarding expectations. She also uses talking points (i.e. focusing on the tasks the clients need to complete) to help keep clients focused.

**Utilize excellent customer service skills
consistently throughout the day
with clients and coworkers.**

CHAPTER NINETEEN

Adapting to Change

Change is constantly occurring within the human services. Some argue that change is one of the few constants in the field and there is much merit to this position. Human service organizations are faced with ongoing challenges to do more with less and to adjust to changing priorities from state agencies. Effective human professionals anticipate change and are able to adjust when changes occur.

Examples of Change
- New database
- New forms
- New process
- New or different responsibilities
- Staff changes (coworker and/or supervisor)
- Sudden and unexpected changes (employee terminations, client discharges, etc.)
- Changes in laws or contracts (different client criteria, different length of contact time with client, etc.)

Responses to Change
- Change or anticipated change typically produces a great deal of anxiety in many people. The human services field is constantly changing and it is vital to understand that change is part of the process and adaptation is essential to survival.

- In one organization many employees left when computers were first introduced due to the high level of anxiety and uncertainty associated with using new technology.

Other common responses include:
- Fear of failure
- Fear of the unknown
- Fear of increased workload
- Fear of potentially losing one's job
- Resistance

Effectively Adapting to Change

- Accept that change is a normal part of life. Change is going to happen with or without your approval so it is important to understand that new information is going to be communicated to you from time to time and to be ready-sometimes with little notice is provided.
  - Allison was just informed that the organization would be using new software for recording client visits on their cell phones. While she was unsure of what this would entail she volunteered to be one of the first case managers to test the new product so that she could have as much time as possible to adapt to the new process.
- Be flexible and open to the new possibilities that change may bring. Change can sometimes be needed.
  - Natasha was nervous when her supervisor announced that she would be leaving the organization. She had worked for her current supervisor for five years and felt very comfortable with her approach. There were rumors that a specific person was going to be promoted and that they were going to be tough to work for. Natasha patiently waited for the new supervisor to be hired and once they came on board she made it a point to meet with them proactively, introduce herself, and ask what was their approach/what they were looking for from their staff. After meeting with the new supervisor

Natasha felt very comfortable with their approach and she was able to focus on her work.

- Manage your anxiety. Some are afraid of change because it disrupts the routine that is in place. However, it is best to proactively address the change as soon as it is announced so that your anxiety can be lowered. Do not jump to conclusions that you will be laid off or transferred due to change. In the event that you are transferred look to the opportunity as a much needed challenge and remain optimistic.
- Self-care is important. Change can create stress and it is vital to take care of yourself, especially during periods of change.
  - Ronnie found himself stressed out with the pending changes within his department/agency. He was worried with his ability to adapt to a new database due to his comfort level with the old one. He often found walking after work and during his lunch break to be a way to reduce stress and clear his head.
- Remain positive. Gossip can quickly envelop the department/organization and it is important to lead by example. If others are gossiping about how the change will negatively impact them, offer up a wait and see approach before making a final decision. While it may be difficult to always be positive about change, especially when you are directly impacted, it is good to see it as a challenge and look forward to meeting it head on.
- See the big picture. Workers do not have all of the information that management has at their disposal. Trust that management is making the change(s) for needed reasons and support that the change is necessary.
- Educate yourself. Stay on top of potential changes in technology so that she can be ready in case they happen.

Going Above and Beyond

Janet sees herself as one that can easily adapt to change. She has been with the organization for close to 10 years and has worked for many supervisors during that time. She has also experienced many changes in policies and procedures.

One of her strategies to effectively adapt to change is to embrace it. She recognizes that changes are going to occur whether she agrees with them or not-she made up her mind to be the first to learn about how the changes may impact her and adapts as needed. She loves working with families and ensures that she makes the time necessary to engage them regardless of the changes occurring in her agency.

**See change as an opportunity
for learning and growth.**

CHAPTER TWENTY

Ethical Standards for Human Service Professionals

Ethics provide guidance and a framework for high quality care. A standard of conduct is necessary to provide guidance in terms of professional behavior. While there are ongoing priorities to meet client needs one should never lose sight of the guiding principles of ethical decision making.

Ethical Standards for Human Service Professionals

The National Organization for Human Services (www.nationalhumanservices.org) provides 54 statements that cover a wide range of ethical and professional expectations for human service professionals. A complete listing of all 54 standards can be found at http://www.nationalhumanservices.org/ethical-standards-for-hs-professionals

Several are listed below:

- Treat each client with respect and dignity at all times.
- Respect the client's right to privacy and confidentiality and protect the integrity, safety and security of all client records.
- Recognize that the power and status of professional to client relationships are unequal and that dual relationships may increase harm to clients.
- Sexual relationships with current clients are not considered to be in the best interest of the client.
- Recognize and build upon client strengths

- Accurately describing the effectiveness of programs and treatments accurately.
- Human service professions are knowledgeable about the cultures and communities within which they practice.
- Remain mindful of your cultural background, beliefs, values, and recognizing the potential for impact on relationships with others.
- Seek training, experience, education and supervision necessary to ensure effectiveness when working with culturally diverse clients.
- When having a conflict with a colleague first seek out that person in an attempt to manage the problem. Involve their supervisory if necessary.
- Know limit and scope of professional knowledge and offer services only within your knowledge and skill base.

Other Ethical Situations to Consider

- Accuracy of records. At all times human service professionals need to ensure that all documentation is factual. There may be times when one is overwhelmed with work priorities but at no time should this involve providing inaccurate or false information like:
  - Falsifying home visits (stating that you were there when you were not)
  - Falsifying mileage reports
  - Misquoting clients to support your position
- Speak to your supervisor before placing yourself in a position where fraud may occur. If you get behind and will not meet deadlines it is better to discuss your situation with your supervisor instead of engaging in fraudulent activity. Once your agency finds out about unethical behavior it typically leads to termination and possibly criminal action (depending on the severity of the action).
  - Larry was overwhelmed at work. He had received several new cases during the month in addition to his already demanding caseload. He was required to visit all of his families at least one time a month and with a few days left he still had several to visit and no

plan on how to accomplish this task. He spoke to his supervisor about the situation and they offered to help complete other tasks for Larry so that he would have enough time to see his families before the end of the month.

- Be a team player but do not cover up for others. If you find out that one of your colleagues is engaging in unethical behavior it is important to discuss the situation with your colleague when possible or discuss it with your supervisor.
  - Natalie was asked to cover Diana's caseload while she was on vacation. Natalie was conducting a visit with one of Diana's clients and was discussing a recent visit that Diana noted in the case file. The client reported that she had not seen or spoke to Diana in approximately two months despite several entries indicating visits to the client's home. Natalie confirmed the last date the client saw Diana and she spoke to Diana upon her return from vacation. Natalie asked Diana about the discrepancy and Diana reported that she was behind in her visits and sometimes "makes up" the visits to reach her monthly quota. Natalie advised Diana that she, Diana, would need to inform the supervisor of the issue, if not, she would. Diana reported that she would not do that because she would be fired so Natalie informed the supervisor. After an investigation it was found fraudulent documentation occurred on several occasions and Diana was terminated.
- Use of self-disclosure: Self-disclosure can be an empowering tool to use when a client is having difficulty working through a situation. However, be careful to not lean on your personal experience too much as it can change the dynamics of the relationship. Also, just because one has personal experience with a situation it does not mean it will help the client. Lastly, be mindful to not share too much personal information with a client or use self-disclosure to build rapport. Remember, clients are not bound by confidentiality.

Going Above and Beyond

Addie believes in consistently utilizing a highly ethical approach to working in the field. She documents to the minute what time she arrives at a client's home as well as when she leaves. She will always budget enough time to complete her work and if she feels that she may have an issue she immediately informs her supervisor. Her mileage records are always accurate and she makes it a habit to write down what others tell her so that she documents all of the facts.

Effective professionals remain mindful to utilize an ethical decision making approach.

CHAPTER TWENTY ONE

Self-Reflection

One of the most important factors in professional growth is self-reflection. Self-reflection involves the ability to observe your behavior and thought process and to critique your performance. Effective human service professionals are mindful about their values and biases and how they may impact their relationships with others.

What Self-Reflection Is
- An internal dialogue of thinking about what happened, why it occurred, and what else you could have done to improve upon the situation.
- Analyzing your actions, decisions, and behaviors.
- Use of critical thinking to assess your performance.
- An ongoing process of examining your professional behavior and routine.
- Understanding your role in the outcome of events (whether positive or negative).

Examples of Self-Reflection
- Analyze interactions with colleagues, clients, and others.
  - Mariana got into an argument with a colleague regarding the best way to engage a pregnant teen who was at risk for losing her child. After careful thought about the conversation she approached the colleague the following day to discuss the conversation again.

Mariana started off the conversation by apologizing for her behavior and stated that she had time to think about their discussion and appreciated the viewpoint that they were trying to make.

- Steve was unsure why one of his clients had not returned his phone calls during a two week period. He visited them at their home to discuss what was going on and found that the client was very defensive and provided short answers to his questions. Steve took a step back during the conversation and thought about their last interaction when he had to tell them about how a specific benefit would be denied if they did not complete a specific task. Steve asked if there was anything that he did that upset them and the client indicated that she was upset with the manner in which he spoke during their last visit. Steve took responsibility for his behavior and apologized.
- Be mindful of your worldview and this may impact your work with clients.
  - Stacey was raised in an upper middle class lifestyle and this meant living in a nice home with a maid and her parents buying her a car when she turned 16. It also meant access to prominent schools and other programs. When she chose to work in the human services she was faced with a culture shock when a roach ran up her leg during a home visit. Stacey had to quickly understand that her families were still good people even though they may not own brand new items and their homes may not be as clean as what she was used to in her lifestyle/upbringing.
- Reflection equals learning, development and growth. When you take time to reflect on your performance you are challenging yourself to improve.

How to Maximize Self-Reflection and Professional Performance

- Keep a journal and actively write. A journal is a key piece of maximizing self-reflection. Writing in a journal allows you to express your innermost thoughts after an empowering day or after a day where you struggled. It also allows you to process the various emotions that you may experience in working with others and to give yourself feedback on how to improve for future situations.

- Irene writes in her journal at least once a week. She takes the opportunity to reflect on the events of the week (personal and professional) and highlights what went well in addition to areas of opportunity. When writing in her journal she feels that she can be honest and freely express fears, concerns, as well as praise when she is able to help a client. She also likes how she can revisit entries for perspective.
- Utilize a critical thinking approach with your performance. Continuously assess your performance in any situation and look for ways that you could have performed differently.
  - After leaving court Mona had much to think about. The hearing did not go the way that she thought it would and she was frustrated with the judge's decision. She thought about her performance during the hearing and determined that if she would have presented the information about the family differently the judge may have ruled in her favor.
- Make time for self-reflection. The world is a busy and demanding place. There are phone calls to return, emails to respond to, paperwork to complete, etc. However, effective professionals are able to find time where they can reflect on their performance and gain insight about their professional behavior.
  - Jamie uses her ride home every evening to reflect on the events of the day. There are times when she turns off the radio so that she can have a few moments to help with clarity and perspective and to assess how she performed in specific situations.
- Align behavior with values and beliefs. Everyone possesses specific values and beliefs and this can be an advantage or a potential barrier that holds us back. Be aware of what your values and beliefs are about others and ensure that they are aligned with professional behavior.

- Be open to change. With self-reflection you may find the need to change or modify an approach with others, which is fine. Human service professionals encourage and motivate clients to expand their skill base and it is important to lead by example.
- Understand your role in the outcome of situations. In every event you should be able to see how your role contributed to the outcome. If the outcome was positive then you should be able to see how you contributed to that. Also, if the outcome was not positive you should be able to see your role and reflect on what you could have done differently.

Going Above and Beyond

Carmen often finds herself thinking about situations and processing the events that occurred and what she did well in addition to what she could have done differently. She takes time to carefully reflect on meetings with clients, her supervisor, and other professionals and to analyze her performance. She has been able to quickly make corrections when she has struggled in an area before her supervisor has had to instruct her.

Self-reflection drives long-term personal and professional growth and leads to optimal client care.

Final Thoughts

Working in the human services is a highly rewarding opportunity. It is also one that can be stressful and frustrating at times. The difference that you want to make is sometimes limited due to funding, eligibility, or resource issues. Still, everyone can choose to make a positive impact everyday regardless of the challenges that are present.

A Few Final Thoughts

- Take ownership of your work, development and future. There will be challenges along the way including but not limited to: unsupportive supervisor, rigid policies/procedures, lack of resources to help clients, etc. Do not allow those challenges to derail your focus on making a difference. You are in control of where your future and career go-do not rely on or blame others.
- Give a high level of effort every day. Some days it will be difficult to excel due to feeling tired, sick, etc. Make it a habit to give your best and go above and beyond when you can. Clients always deserve your best effort and so does your department and agency.
- Build and strengthen relationships with others. Relationships are critical to your success as a human service professional and having strong connections with other professionals, in your organization and in the community is vital to meeting client needs and helping you to navigate the many systems involved in client care.

- Keep learning. Never stop growing and looking for opportunities to expand your knowledge base and skill set. Look for books, articles, and online resources to help guide your ongoing commitment to helping others.
- Do not assume. Use critical thinking skills to find out as much information as possible. Remember the difference between thinking versus knowing and how that can potentially impact your credibility as a human service professional.
- Freely share information with others. If you find a resource that works do not hesitate to share with others. Some like to keep as much information to themselves as possible and this does not benefit the organization.
- Be flexible and adaptive. Change is continuously occurring in the human services. Those that can embrace change stand to experience lower levels of stress and higher job satisfaction. Also, remain flexible with your beliefs and values-clients come from all walks of life and they do not deserve to be judged.
- Use humor. One of the keys to a long and fulfilling career is the ability to laugh throughout the day and to not take things too seriously. Have fun-the job can be very serious at times and secondary trauma is a real concern in some sectors of the field. Be mindful to minimize the personal impact working in the field can have on you.
- Make an active commitment toward self-care. If you do not take care of yourself, it will be difficult to take care of others.
- Seek out support. Others within your agency and community are experiencing the same levels of stress as you. Seek out others that have positive solutions and are actively working on making their work environment a better and more supportive place.
- Ask questions. Use open-ended questions with all individuals that you encounter. This helps to broaden the depth of relationships as well as to obtain vital information and feedback to expand your knowledge, skills and relationships.

- Always attempt to see where others are coming from. Use empathy in all interactions with clients and other professionals. Take a moment to reflect on why the person believes what they do and truly attempt to see their points. Clients have many challenges and sometimes they need an understanding ally.
- Follow through. When you make a commitment to accomplish a task be sure to complete it within that timeframe or earlier if possible. Your professional reputation is comprised of actions not words.
- Remember why you chose to work in the human services. Do not lose sight of your passion for helping others and making a difference. Take a day off from time to time to reconnect with your personal mission for working in the field.
- Learn from your clients and colleagues. Every interaction is an opportunity to learn something that you can use to better yourself and improve your performance.
- Use self-reflection. Self-reflection is a key ingredient to being a highly effective human service professional. Be active in processing events that occur throughout the day and look for opportunities for growth and improvement.
- Choose to be a "make it happen" professional. Be creative and find ways to meet client needs regardless of challenges and barriers.

About the Author

Tim Nolan has worked in the human services for over 10 years and is the coauthor of *The Essential Handbook for Human Service Leaders*. In 2011 he founded The Human Services Leadership Institute and travels the country providing leadership development workshops and organizational consultation. He has provided leadership training to nearly 1,500 managers. In addition to providing training and consultation to human service organizations, Tim has been a faculty member with the University of Phoenix since 2009. He teaches various undergraduate courses in the human services and is a subject matter expert where he has helped to develop and redesign several classes.

Tim lives in Lake Worth, Florida with his wife and daughter.

Tim can be reached at Tim@HumanServicesLeadership.org

CPSIA information can be obtained at www.ICGtesting.com
Printed in the USA
LVOW05s1237100414

381151LV00005B/309/P